REFLECTIONS

THE ART OF STEPHEN BRADBURY

To John and Ailsa
God bless
and best wishes
Stephen Bradbury

REFLECTIONS

THE ART OF STEPHEN BRADBURY

Text By David J. Howe

To Sue with great love
& Rachael, Hope and Jonathon

Paper Tiger
An Imprint of Dragon's World
Dragon's World Ltd
Limpsfield, Surrey RH8 0DY
Great Britain

First Published by Dragon's World Ltd 1996

The catalogue record for this book is available from the British Library
ISBN 1 85028 339 7 Limpback

Editor Philip Wilkinson
Designer Nigel Coath at ProCreative
Art Director John Strange
Editorial Director Pippa Rubinstein

Printed in Singapore

Page 1

The Grey Horse 1988
Poster Colours
340 x 310mm
Cover for The Grey Horse
by R. A. MacAvoy
Bantam Books

The Grey Horse is set in Ireland and it isn't a straightforward fantasy book. The sandpipers on the paintings are based on the sort of bird that we see on the Lizard Peninsula all the time. The original for this painting was damaged and I therefore had to cut it down to the portion that is reproduced here.

Page 2

Greenthieves 1994
Gouache
455 x 290mm
Cover for Greenthieves
by Alan Dean Foster
Orbit Books

This was a detective story set in the future and it was like a comedy of errors. I tried to include a lot of detail in the undergrowth to suggest the humorous nature of the book. The picture has also been designed to make you look at the two figures, everything points towards them at the centre of the painting.

CONTENTS

1

INTRODUCTION

— *Mirage Fantasy* —

Stephen Bradbury has, over the last 15 years, provided evocative and inspired paintings for the covers of a wide selection of fantasy and horror fiction. This book collects together just some of his work. There are paintings from an early project, *The Chronicles of Time*, we look at the groundbreaking covers for Julian May's fantasy series *The Saga of the Exiles* and explore fantastic landscapes, creatures, sorcerers and beautiful maidens. Also presented are examples of private, previously unpublished work. Welcome to the worlds of Stephen Bradbury.

The Way Of Wyrd 1984

Poster Colours
405 x 260mm
Cover for The Way of Wyrd
by Brian Bates, Century Books

This was one of my earliest book covers and one of my favourites. It's about pagan times in Britain and the clash between real-time religion and paganism. I tried to keep the cover as simple as possible by using the bird as a centrepiece. It was also the first time that I attempted to use a light-source from somewhere other than in the sky, in this case it is coming from the sword.

The Black Dragon 1987

Poster Colours
190 x 360mm
Insert picture for Tea With The Black Dragon
by R. A. MacAvoy, Bantam Books

This picture went at the top of the book cover. The book was based on an old Chinese legend about a black dragon who woke up one day to find that he was an old Chinese wise man. The man then goes to America and becomes a detective. What I wanted to do with the insert was to show the Chinese side of the story, while the main picture (see page 16) was of the American side.

S
B

As a child, influences can come from many sources, and the first books that Stephen Bradbury can remember reading featured the legends of King Arthur and the Round Table. These myths and stories have continued to fascinate the artist and the themes and imagery of loyal knights, trusty steeds, beautiful maidens and sword-like icons of power are represented in much of his work, even right from the start. 'When I started painting at school, these Arthurian legends were my chosen subject matter,' he explained. 'I was also inspired and fascinated by the work of H. G. Wells and Arthur Conan Doyle.

'According to my mother, I was painting my own landscapes and creations in oils when I was aged seven or eight. I then started winning local prizes and my teacher at grammar school was encouraging me to paint more and more.'

At the age of 15, Stephen started to become interested in other things – mainly cars, bikes and girls – and his artistic

Mullion Cove 1995
Gouache
400 x 280mm
Original for this collection

I painted this landscape especially for this collection and it is very similar to those I complete for commercial sale. For me this view is the perfect view on Earth. Of all the places I've been to, this is the one place I really feel at home. This view is about a mile from my house and I can sit for hours, watching the waves crashing against the rocks. The beauty comes from the contours of the cove and these huge rocks jutting out of the sea.

Catch Trap 1988
Poster Colours
400 x 240mm
Cover for Catch Trap by Marion Zimmer Bradley, Sphere Books

This was a difficult book to illustrate, mainly because it wasn't a fantasy book, and was about two gay trapeze artists based in Italy. However the author was known for her fantasy work and so the jacket was given a fantasy feel. At the time I had a great sense of satisfaction at having cracked the problem.

The Best Of Marion Zimmer Bradley 1990

Gouache
Back Cover 280 x 220mm
Front Cover 380 x 240mm
From The Best of Marion Zimmer Bradley edited by Martin H. Greenberg, Sphere Books

The paintings are simply made up of all the things from the stories in the book combined together. It was a very difficult cover to do as I didn't want to take one story as the subject for the cover, and trying to combine everything together was something of a design nightmare. The book also featured stories that were both science fiction and fantasy so there was a mixture of elements to include as well.

subject matter changed from works of imagination to pictures of hot-rods and dragsters. This continued until around the age of seventeen.

'I remember for my "A" level project I had to do something on the history of art and I chose surrealism. This really grabbed my attention and shook me up. At about the same time Monty Python's Flying Circus was on the television and this show presented a very surreal view of the world. I started to incorporate this imagery into my paintings. Surrealist art is fantasy art and I have continued with

The Great Divide 1993

Gouache
425 x 300mm
From 'The Garden Series'
Artist's own project
Previously unpublished

During the 1993 recession I was able to spend some time doing my own thing and the pictures in my 'Garden Series' were the result. The Great Divide looks at rich and poor and the division between classes. The idea for the ship came from a ship-building company in Holland, I think, which actually has a ship built into its office.

The Blue Rose 1993

Gouache
425 x 300mm
From 'The Garden Series'
Artist's own project
Previously unpublished

One consistent thing with these pictures are the topiary bushes. I have used the same shapes in several pictures. The Blue Rose is about how humanity spends its time arguing over nothing. The blue rose does not exist in nature, and these two magpies are therefore arguing over possession of a rose that does not exist.

The Ice House 1993

Gouache
480 x 290mm
Cover for The Ice House by
Minette Walters, Pan Books

The Ice House came about after I showed my 'Garden Series' works to Pan Books; a few weeks later they asked me to do the covers for a new series of detective novels, using the topiary idea from The Blue Rose.

The Sculptress 1993

Gouache
470 x 300mm
Cover for The Sculptress by
Minette Walters, Pan Books

This is another detective story and my cover is influenced by Magritte, especially in the sculpture. I started by airbrushing the sky and then hand painting the rest, finishing with the bricks.

Methuselah's Children 1986

Poster Colours
390 x 240mm
Cover for Methuselah's Children by Robert Heinlein, New English Library

The story was about longevity and Methuselah was supposed to be the oldest living human ever. The mountain ranges are very much inspired by the Julian May paintings and the central image of the prism was possibly inspired by Pink Floyd's album cover for Dark Side of the Moon.

Fire Dancer 1987

Poster Colours
460 x 290mm
Cover for Fire Dancer by Anne Maxwell, Orbit Books

The story was about a race of women who could generate fire from their bodies and use it as a weapon. I deliberately painted the woman on the cover as a very sexless being.

Lythande 1988

Poster Colours
345 x 210mm
Front cover for Lythande by Marion Zimmer Bradley, Sphere Books

Lythande was a wizard and the big secret was that she was a woman and not a man. To hide this on the cover I gave her a long robe that hid her legs. The overall theme of the cover is of a hidden danger. The landscape is attractive but there's still a hint of danger.

The Chronicles Of Mavin Manyshaped 1986

Poster Colours
340 x 225mm
Cover for The Chronicles of Mavin Manyshaped by Sheri S. Tepper, Corgi Books

Sheri S. Tepper wrote a series of books based on 'the true game' where everyone had a role as a gamesman. The games board reflects this theme.

The Cards Of Grief 1986

Poster Colours
410 x 245mm
Cover for The Cards of Grief by Jane Yolen, Orbit Books

This was a strange and difficult picture to paint as I had to keep turning it around to paint the same bit twice. The idea was of a playing card with the bottom mirroring the top. It contains small details like the moon waxing in the four corners. The book is about people who have transformed the act of mourning into an art form and people who were truly gifted at grieving were revered. It is a science fiction novel so I included a space helmet on the painting to indicate that. One of the reasons it looks strange is that the images are not reflections of each other, but are also reversed.

Tea With The Black Dragon 1987

Poster Colours
Original size 450 x 280mm
Cover for Tea With The Black Dragon by R. A. MacAvoy, Bantam Books

This is the main picture from the book cover (the insert picture appears on page 7). I feel it is very surreal – think of Magritte's picture of a man with a bowler hat for a head. There had to be a symmetry to the piece, which is set in Seattle, hence the two clock towers on either side of the city-scape across the river. The stars are a bit of a trade mark for me. I seem to include them in quite a few of my pictures.

this thread in my work to the present day; taking the imagery until it goes over the edge so it's quite realistic but not so abstract that you can't relate to it.

'It was while taking my foundation degree course at Bolton in 1973 that my perceptions changed once more. To get to the college from where I lived in Cheshire I had to take a train into Manchester, walk across Manchester and then get another train to Bolton – I read loads of fantasy books on those trains, Michael Moorcock's Elric tales and such like – and I used to stop off each day at Manchester's City Art Gallery. The minute I saw their collection of Pre-Raphaelite paintings I was hooked.

The Dark Tower 1987

Poster Colours
585 x 420mm
Unused cover for
The Dark Tower Volume 1
by Stephen King

The Dark Tower was Stephen King's foray into fantasy. I was commissioned to paint the cover, but by the time I had finished, King and his agent had decided that they wanted to use the same cover on the books globally and so therefore the American cover was going to be used on the UK editions. I don't believe that King ever saw my final cover.

The Tower Of Azgar-Kumar 1995

Pencil sketch
350 x 230mm
Unpublished

Azgar-Kumar was the villain from *The Chronicles of Time* and I always liked the name so when I completed this pencil sketch I decided to use one of the ideas from *The Chronicles of Time* as the theme. The sketch was completed with a very soft 6B pencil, with different pressure and usage creating the different tones, textures and hard lines. It probably took me about an hour to complete.

Whenever I have taught students to paint, one of the first things I get them to do is to just use black and white paint so that they get used to using tones rather than colours. I get them to copy a photograph of a landscape in black and white so that all they have to worry about is the tones. Once they get the hang of the tones, then it is easier to add the colour.

The Lords Of Vaumartin 1990

Gouache
415 x 270mm
Cover for The Lords of Vaumartin by Cecelia Holland, Futura Books

The art director had asked for a medieval style and so I took several characters from the book and painted them accordingly.

There, before my eyes, were all these Arthurian legends brought to vivid life and colour. That to me was how you should paint and ever since then I've had an ambition to be able to paint like the Pre-Raphaelites.'

While he was at Bolton, Stephen's tutors tried to knock this fascination out of him. and by the end of the foundation course he was a bit confused about which direction to take. 'Shortly after starting my degree I became a Christian and I suddenly started wondering why I was doing what I was doing. My whole perception of the value of life changed. I decided to give up the course and got a job as a postman. I stayed as a postman for ten years, but after about nine years, I was overtaken by an incredible urge to start painting again.

'At about this time illustrated book covers were starting to appear on the bookshelves and I decided to write something that I could illustrate myself. This project was called *The Chronicles of Time*. I began to approach publishers and agents, and after several disappointments I tried Pan Books.'

The Rainbow Abyss 1991
Gouache
370 x 515mm
Cover for The Rainbow Abyss by
Barbara Hambly, Grafton Books

Following Page

This is one of my favourite pieces. The novel was about the Nazis trying to evoke powers from another world to help with their search for power.

SB

2

A DISTANT VIEW

— *The Saga of the Exiles* —

The association between best-selling fantasy authoress Julian May and artist Stephen Bradbury came about almost by chance. Having decided to try Pan books as his final port of call on an otherwise disastrous visit to London, Stephen found himself talking to the secretary of Pan's Art Director at the time.

Intervention 1987
Gouache
560 x 330mm (estimated)
Cover for Intervention by Julian May
Harper Collins/Pan Books

Because of the original cover being rejected (see above), I had only four days to do this painting so I worked solidly for two nights without sleep in order to complete it. I tried to get the feeling of a creature going about its ordinary way of life and then its life pattern being interrupted as something intervenes. The original painting was stolen from the publishers so if anyone knows of its whereabouts, please can I have it back?

Arrival 1987
Gouache
510 x 440mm
Unused cover for Intervention by Julian May

This was based on Julian May's own ideas for the book jacket, but because of the nature of the previous covers it wasn't felt suitable by the publishers. The picture shows the spaceships of the Galactic Mileaux arriving to announce themselves to Earth.

The Many Coloured Land 1982

Poster Colours
405 x 245mm
Cover for The Many Coloured Land by Julian May, Pan Books

This was the first book in the series and my first ever book cover. I had only bought my air brush a few months before and this was the first occasion that I had to use it in anger. I also had to learn to use brighter colours as a book cover has to look bright and attractive, and up to that point my paintings had been more muted in their colouring.

'About the first thing she told me was that Gary Day-Ellison didn't see anybody on Fridays and that I would have to come back next week. I explained that I couldn't as I was going back up north. I think my obvious disappointment must have softened her heart because she said that she'd find out if he would see me. She came back shortly and told me that I had five minutes. So I went to see Gary and he started flicking through my portfolio, just like everybody else had done. My hopes were fading fast but then he said, "I haven't seen anybody who can paint like this for years." I

The Golden Torc 1982
Poster Colours
300 x 180mm
Cover for The Golden Torc by Julian May, Pan Books

This was the second book in Julian May's series and was the second book cover I ever completed. Because *The Many Coloured Land* had sold around 100,000 copies, *The Golden Torc* had to follow that up and became a far more important book cover as a result. I managed to follow the same style as the first cover and the book instantly went into the book charts, and my reputation soared literally overnight. It was only my second cover and yet I was almost instantly in demand for more work.

wondered what he meant. Is that good or bad? And he said, "No, I haven't seen anybody who can paint like this, and the mountain you've done here is brilliant." He asked me what I was doing now and I explained that I was literally on my way home back to my job with the Post Office. "We can't have that," he said and reached for a book off his shelf. This was the American edition of Julian May's *The Many Coloured Land*. He told me to take the book home and to do a new cover for it. So I looked at the book, and I looked at Gary and was quite literally speechless. I had

The Non-Born King 1983
Poster Colours
535 x 315mm
Cover for The Non-Born King
by Julian May, Pan Books

The idea here was to paint a picture which kept the surreal nature of the series going and not to portray people. The picture asks the questions: Why is the throne floating? Why is it there?

actually been commissioned!'

Stephen was later to discover that that book had been on Day-Ellison's shelf for about four months. He hadn't been able to think of any illustrator who could come up with what he wanted. When Stephen walked through his door it was like the answer to a prayer. Rushing home, the first thing Stephen did was to sell his motorbike and buy an airbrush.

'On a technical level I knew I needed to use an airbrush for the sky, but I didn't know how to. I also discovered that I needed masking film, different brushes and all sorts of art supplies that I had not used before. I had to learn all these techniques myself overnight in order to complete that first cover. I didn't know anything about the consistency of paint to use with an airbrush or anything about the problems in using the tool, I just had to experiment. In the end it took me about four attempts to get the sky right before I could move onto the rest of the picture.

'I discovered that it is a very different thing wanting to be asked

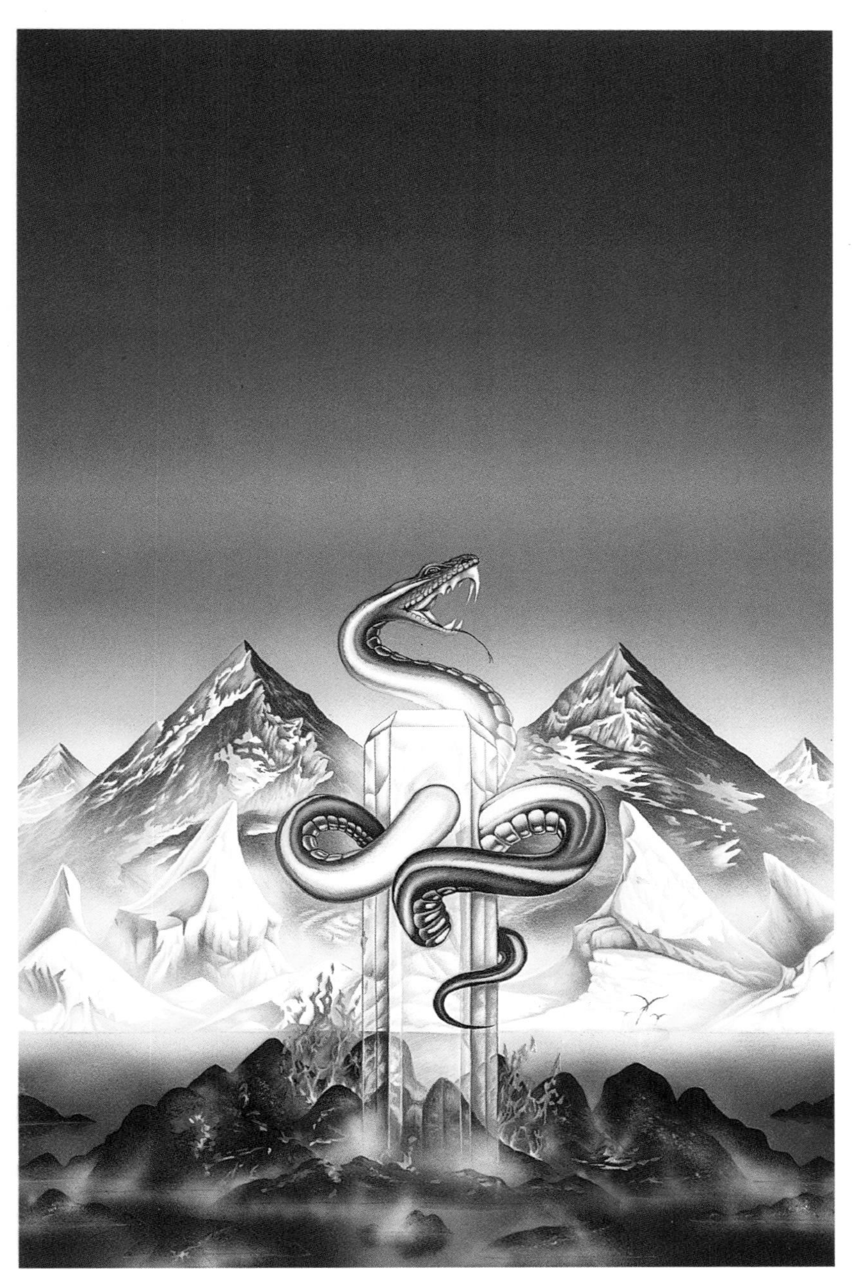

The Adversary 1984

Poster Colours
560 x 330mm
Cover for The Adversary
by Julian May, Pan Books

By this time I was doing the covers up to eighteen months in advance of the book being completed. I would ring Julian up in the States and discuss my ideas with her. For *The Adversary* I told Julian that I wanted to show a snake in a crystal pillar as though it was being gripped by an adversary. I like to use metaphorical images to get a point across rather than something painfully obvious like a man with a sword. As a result of this Julian included a snake in the book, so I like to think that perhaps my imagery has influenced the series to some small degree.

Jack The Bodiless 1991

Gouache
420 x 285mm
Cover for US Edition of Jack The Bodiless by Julian May, Knopf

Following Page

The Americans have a different approach to the book covers than in the UK. The brief here was to just show the character Jack who is in the background. I added the three birds flying above the water to try and tie it in with the British edition. The landscape is supposed to evoke the area around Mount Washington.

Jack The Bodiless 1991
Gouache
460 x 285mm
Cover for UK Edition of Jack The Bodiless by Julian May
HarperCollins/Pan Books
Previous Page

This carries on the theme from *Intervention* with the crystal shattering. The globe signifies the birth of Jack. Half the globe is the Earth and the other half is the embryonic Jack. The eyes in the sky on this version of the painting are of the character Fury who is the main protagonist.

to do something and buckling down to actually doing it. Working on *The Many Coloured Land* taught me the true reality of working to a deadline. The painting had to be completed within a week or so, and it really got scary. I didn't know at the time that this was going to be the first in a series of novels and therefore that first cover was created as a one-off. I have to admit that I really didn't have a clue what I was doing! The publishers had asked me for a more landscape orientated look to the fantasy rather than something out of Conan the Barbarian – muscled men and beautiful women in peril. I therefore came up with the idea of a landscape and we decided to place an object – a dinosaur-like skull – in front. The story is based six million years ago when no humans were supposed to be around, and the skull was painted so that it looked as though it had been deliberately placed there, except, of course, that it couldn't have been.'

Shortly after delivering the first picture, Stephen was commissioned to do the second, *The Golden Torc*, and again he had very little time in which to complete it. 'Fortunately something just clicked. I think at the time a lot of it was instinctive, and we ended up with a series of paintings that looked as though they had been planned as a series.

'Julian May's books are very layered and are quite demanding to the reader. In the final book in the series, *Magnificat*, Julian has taken the series full circle and has ended up right back at the start of *The Many Coloured Land*!

'Just as the books have followed a pattern, I have incorporated a pattern into the cover paintings for the second part of the series. I have metamorphosed the cover picture as the series continued. So the diamond shape shatters and becomes a sphere (*Jack The Bodiless*), the sphere lands and shatters and turns into an angel (*Diamond Mask*) and, finally, the angel metamorphoses back into the skull which was featured on *The Many Coloured Land*, and the reflection in the water is also from that first book (*Magnificat*).

Diamond Mask 1994
Gouache
470 x 280mm
Cover for Diamond Mask by Julian May, HarperCollins/Pan Books

The globe lands and shatters to reveal an angel. Jack can take on any shape or form and one of the characters, Marc Remillard, is described somewhere in the book as the angel of the abyss. The eyes in the sky are of a character called Dorothea Macdonald who is known as 'Diamond Mask'.

3

MIRROR IMAGES

— Heroes & Heroines —

It is inevitable that at some point a Fantasy artist will be called upon to create the muscled and strongly heroic male, and the lissom and lithe, long-haired female. In fact, these two stereotypes have become increasingly blurred, and today it is as often the female who wields the double-edged sword while the innocent man cowers from the foraging dragon.

The First Name 1986
Poster Colours
480 x 270mm
Cover for The First Name by Dennis Schmidt, Orbit Books

This was the first cover on which I painted a humanoid figure. I included a giant tree of life in the background which changed as the series of books progressed. I based the figure on Michaelangelo's 'David'. This fusion of figures and landscapes was very popular at the time.

A Spell Of Empire 1992
Gouache
480 x 270mm
Cover for A Spell of Empire by Michael Scott Rohan and Allan Scott, Orbit Books

The brief here was to portray all four characters from the story on the cover in a fairly defined pose. I had great fun inventing the buildings on the left of the picture.

‘The first cover I completed which featured a human character was Dennis Schmidt’s *The First Name*, and I had to learn to paint figures pretty fast. I find people harder to paint than landscapes as with a figure you can’t get away with as much as you can when painting a landscape. A figure has to look right, all the elements have to be there in the right places: hands, feet, fingers and so on. Sometimes you cheat and engineer the design of the painting to remove the hands: maybe the character is holding a wreath of flowers, maybe they are standing behind a horse, or have their hands in their lap as they lean against a tree. I have painted covers for a lot of romantic fiction, where the requirement is for figures to look almost photographic in their realism, and as this is what is required for the piece, then that is what you have to do.’

Stephen has a specific approach to painting with which he tackles every work.

‘When painting figures I have to have a starting point. I either get someone to stand in the appropriate position, or I use a copy scanner which is basically like a photographic enlarger. You place a small reference picture or photograph under the glass at the bottom, and then you project an image of that picture up onto a sheet of tracing paper at the top. By adjusting the height of the upper plate you can alter the size of the final image which you then trace. I initially complete my roughs to the same size as the finished book, then, once that has been agreed, I use the copy

Dragonslayer 1994
Gouache
305 x 310mm
Unpublished

This was my attempt at a Conan-type figure and it was really just to see if I could do it. There was also the fact that I wanted to try and attract American publishers to my work and they seemed to like this kind of heroic figure.

SB

scanner to enlarge the rough to form the basis for the final painting. I feel that an illustrator is lost without a copy scanner. It makes life so much easier!

'When working on any painting, I always start with the rough. This is a pencil or ink sketch which is completed to show whoever has commissioned me what the final painting will look like. It contains all the elements of the final piece, but just loosely sketched in to show the arrangement: where the people will be, where the mountains will be and so on. The next stage is to transfer that rough sketch to a sheet of art board. That is done

Rosig 1981
Poster Colours
300 x 370mm
From The Chronicles of Time.
Author's own project
Previously unpublished

It was the mountain in the background to this painting that impressed Gary Day-Ellison at Pan to commission me for *The Many Coloured Land*.

Ritnym's Daughter 1990
Gouache
505 x 335mm
Cover for Ritnym's Daughter by Sheila Gilluly, Headline Books

This was the sequel to Sheila Gilluly's *Greenbriar Queen* and therefore the cover had to be in the same style. I had wanted to use a beam of light shooting into the sky from a tower in a painting somewhere and it ended up being used on this cover. There are three ships in the bottom centre panel as I was reminded of the popular carol 'I Saw Three Ships'.

The Golden Bell 1981
Poster Colours
560 x 450mm
From The Chronicles of Time.
Author's own project
Previously unpublished

The person on the horse is the main character in the story and the Merlin-like character is carrying the seashell-shaped golden bell. The style of grass and landscape was heavily influenced by an illustrator called Kay Nielsen.

using the copy scanner.

'After I have the rough sketch transferred to the art board, I then tackle the painting from the most distant item to the closest, in that order. Therefore the sky is always the first thing that I paint. To do that I first use masking film to mask off all the elements of the picture that are not sky – any mountains, trees that may extend up against the sky, people, birds and so forth are all masked off. This can take some time as each element has to be carefully cut around with a scalpel to leave the sky showing.

'Once I have everything but the sky masked, I then use the airbrush to lay down the colour for the sky. This is done by applying the lighter colours first and then working towards the darker colours. In this way you build up the image and colour in layers, resulting in a glowing, vibrant feel to the painting.

The Destiny Of The Sword 1991
Gouache
465 x 295mm
Cover for The Destiny of the Sword by Dave Duncan, Legend Books

This was the third book in the series. To get a series look I had decided to use a border where the image outside the frame was a slightly different colour as though it was being seen through a filter. In the far distance I placed a massive waterfall in the sky in order to make the picture more interesting.

The Horse Lord 1983
Poster Colours
320 x 470mm
Cover for The Horse Lord by
Peter Morwood, Century Books

The Horse Lord is set in a really cold landscape where realistically anyone in armour would freeze to death. The image here was dictated by the book's title which was too strong to depict anything else. I had recently seen the film Star Wars for the first time and so the helmet of the rider was influenced by the look of Darth Vader from the film.

The Crystal Keep 1989

Gouache
505 x 335mm
Cover for The Crystal Keep by Sheila Gilluly, Headline Books

This was the second book in a trilogy. I had developed a series design involving panels which though a good way of introducing different characters from the story, were very difficult to mask and keep clean while I was working on the rest of the painting. The picture depicts Queen Ariadne. She is arriving at the Crystal Keep, which is locked in deep snow and ice right at the edge of the world.

Dervish Daughter 1988

Gouache
480 x 295mm
Cover for Dervish Daughter by Sheri S. Tepper, Corgi Books

The cover does not depict an exact happening from the book; but it gives the reader an idea of what is going on. The plot concerns a heroine called Jinian Footseer and in this painting she is wielding the dagger of Daggerhawk Demesne. This commission introduced a more hard-edged style for me which, although it felt alien to me as a painter, has proved very successful and popular. I subsequently used this style for quite a few years.

Jinian Star Eye 1988

Gouache
480 x 290mm
Cover for Jinian Star Eye by Sheri S. Tepper, Corgi Books

This was the final cover for the Jinian trilogy and our heroine is looking down on the Shadowtower as demons are conjured to attack her. It seemed that Jinian became more Amazonian with each successive picture – she was having trouble keeping her clothes on.

S
B

The Citadel Of Autarch 1990

Gouache
345 x 525mm
Cover for The Citadel of Autarch
by Gene Wolfe, Legend Books

Previous Page

This was the fourth in a series. The dark broodiness of the picture is supposed to represent the devouring blackness gnawing at the heart of the old sun. The main character pictured here is Severian, an apprentice torturer.

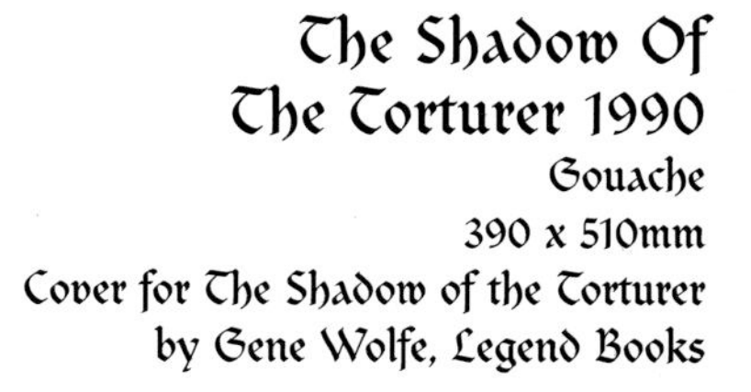

The Shadow Of The Torturer 1990

Gouache
390 x 510mm
Cover for The Shadow of the Torturer
by Gene Wolfe, Legend Books

This was the first book in a series and many of the images on the cover come from the landscape in the High Peaks of Derbyshire. The citadel on the front was based on a large church organ which I adapted to make it more building-like.

Jinian Footseer 1988
Poster Colours
345 x 230mm
Cover for Jinian Footseer by
Sheri S. Tepper, Corgi Books

The first few Sheri S. Tepper books that I painted covers for had definite archways featured on them. As we progressed, little by little, we got rid of the archways. Here, only the top remains. The main character, Jinian, is quite well dressed here compared with how she ends up in later paintings.

The Giant Of Inishkerry 1992
Gouache
430 x 370mm
Cover for The Giant of Inishkerry by Sheila Gilluly
Headline Books

There isn't a giant on the picture because I was only given a paragraph of text and a brief description of which characters to put on the front – like, for example, a one-legged dwarf. The border and geometry at the top were for the series look and the flowers were to tie in with Gilluly's previous series. I was especially pleased with the lighting on the mountains at the back.

'I always have a vague idea of what colours the sky should be, and once that is complete, it dictates the colours of the rest of the picture: if it's a pinkish sky then there will be pinkish hues on the landscape. If you do a blue sky, then the mountains will also be in shades of blue. In a way you can't use realistic colour references because you don't get skies or landscapes in those fantastic colours.

'Once the sky has been completed, I then use a scalpel to carefully cut out the next farthest images – perhaps the

The Twilight Of The Serpent 1987
Poster Colours
390 x 240mm
Cover for The Twilight of the Serpent by Peter Valentine Timlett, Orbit Books

The picture shows the sun going down on the druids. In the foreground is a cup-like chalice which represents Christianity coming in. I had just moved to Cornwall when this picture was commissioned and so the landscape is my first attempt at a Cornish scene.

The Firebrand 1994
Gouache
400 x 575mm
Cover for The Firebrand by Marion Zimmer Bradley, Penguin Books

The Firebrand is based at the time of the fall of Troy, and I've messed around with the landscape quite a lot. The serpent does appear in the story but I've accentuated it and made it a lot bigger. I also made the character on the cover more of a fantasy female than perhaps a Trojan woman would have looked, but then again I've not seen many Trojan women.

mountains – and peel the masking film off to reveal the board beneath. Then I use very fine brushes and paint to create the elements of the picture, slowly coming forward until the final element – usually the focus of the picture, but not always – is completed.

'This technique can be very scary because, if, for example, you are doing a painting in which a person is the focus, then that person ends up being the last thing you paint. I can't say I'm the

The Mists Of Avalon 1993
Gouache
330 x 535mm
Cover for The Mists of Avalon
by Marion Zimmer Bradley
Penguin Books

The Mists of Avalon was set in Cornwall and was an Arthurian adventure, therefore the cover reflected those elements. The scenery is of the view towards St Michael's Mount and the figure on the horse is a typical Pre-Raphaelite woman.

world's greatest figure painter and by the time you get to the last few inches and you've got to paint somebody's face, you've spent maybe ten days on the background. This then sets you thinking that if something goes wrong now, then ten days' work has been wasted. You can't cough or

Wintermind 1987

Poster Colours
475 x 295mm
Cover for Wintermind
by Marvin Kay and Parke
Godwin, Orbit Books

Wintermind and *The Mists of Avalon* show the contrast between two paintings which feature the same elements. *Wintermind* is set in the barbaric future and the girl here is a wild female barbarian. The stretched bearskin on the left was a device on which text could be placed on the final cover.

The Claw Of The Conciliator 1990

Gouache
345 x 525mm
Cover for The Claw of the Conciliator by Gene Wolfe
Legend Books

Following Page

The landscape here is based on Scotland and the Claw of the Conciliator is actually the crystal being held by the woman in the foreground. The castle has been inspired by Burmese architecture with the rounded spikes on the peaks of the towers.

Magicians Of The Night 1992

Gouache
380 x 510mm
Cover for Magicians of the Night by Barbara Hambly
Grafton Books

This was the sequel to *The Rainbow Abyss* and again uses the image of an eagle carrying a swastika. The scenery here is of a more realistic world than the first picture in the series.

SB

Wizard Of The Pigeons 1987
Poster Colours
340 x 435mm
Cover for Wizard of the Pigeons
by Megan Lindholm, Corgi Books

Megan Lindholm's *Wizard of the Pigeons* was the first cover I did after having discovered the American artist Maxfield Parrish. At the turn of the century he was doing staggering landscapes and surreal images that were way ahead of their time. All the fantasy illustrators working today have been influenced by his work, even if they haven't seen it directly. When I discovered Parrish my idea of art changed overnight.

The Gate To Women's Country 1989
Gouache
475 x 295mm
Cover for The Gate to Women's Country
by Sheri S. Tepper, Bantam Press

I was criticised for including the horsemen in this picture as they didn't exist in the world I was painting. There is a smiley crab under the roots of the tree on the left hand side which was included as part of a running joke between myself and the designer. No-one ever noticed these inclusions at the time.

sneeze in case you inadvertently mark the painted background; it's a worrying business.

'The technique of building up the colours by moving from light to dark is the way everything in the picture is completed. For example, for a face, I start by painting it white, then slowly build up to whatever flesh tone seems appropriate for the painting and for the character. Laying down this initial colour also helps because the art boards are slightly absorbent and the first layer soaks in. After that you find that the paint goes on much quicker and easier and builds up to give the completed image.

'I use gentle and small diagonal brush

The Boy From The Burren 1991
Gouache
370 x 230mm
Back Cover for The Boy from the Burren by Sheila Gilluly, Headline Books

strokes to fill in the fine detail. And of course the secret is not to show the brush strokes, which is quite difficult. One of the reasons why I limit my use of the airbrush to the sky is that if you overuse it then you can lose the personality of the painting. Airbrush manuals will say that you can use

airbrushing all the time but a painting by one airbrush artist looks very similar to a painting by another. I like to believe that people are commissioning me because they like my style, which is all done with the hand. If I were to give any advice at all to prospective illustrators, then it would

The Boy From The Burren 1991
Gouache
370 x 230mm
Front Cover for The Boy from the Burren by Sheila Gilluly
Headline Books

These two pictures give a full view of the world in which the character is standing, showing what is in front of and behind him. The brooch on his chest is my logo which I like to include in my pictures.

S
B

The Emperor Of Earth Above 1993
Gouache
430 x 370mm
Cover for The Emperor of Earth Above by Sheila Gilluly
Headline Books

Previous Page

I had a very short brief for this painting, consisting only of descriptions of the characters. They have just been shipwrecked which is why they look unhappy.

Greenbriar Queen 1989
Gouache
505 x 335mm
Cover for Greenbriar Queen by Sheila Gilluly, Headline Books

Previous Page

Sheila Gilluly's covers turned out to be something of a nightmare to paint because I had decided to use a flower motif around the border. I cut round all those flowers individually with a scalpel so I could leave them clean as well as leaving masking film on the borders. The last thing I did was to peel off the thin white line hoping that no paint had got in underneath it. Luckily for most of the time it works out fine, and when it doesn't, then there is no option but to reach for the pot of white paint and to try and clean up those little fine lines. I suppose over the years this is one of the aspects of painting that you master.

The Kingmaking 1995
Gouache
395 x 585mm
Cover for The Kingmaking by Helen Hollick
Mandarin Books

This painting was very much inspired by John Waterhouse and the Pre-Raphaelites. Whereas he had six months to complete a piece I had six days.

simply be that the important thing is to have good ideas. Very often when painting book covers I've just had the title of the book, or, on occasion, not even that much! But instantly my mind can see it, and I just scribble down what my mind is seeing. I suppose that's my gift really. I can come up with an idea within a few minutes, or even five ideas for the same picture. When you consider book covers, they are a rectangular shape, they never

vary. You know that the top third of the painting will have the book's title over it and the bottom two thirds is yours to play with. Given these parameters, if you can think of many ways to twist that book cover around then you're going to do well.'

4

SHADOWS

— Villains —

Villains in fantasy come in all different shapes and sizes. There are dragons and ogres, mischievous elves, dark wizards and evil witch queens. There are also villains that you can't see, intangible creatures of mist and smoke, elementals that can take any form.

The Bones Of The Moon 1988
Poster Colours
450 x 275mm
Unused cover for The Bones of the Moon by Jonathan Carroll

The novel was not really a fantasy book, it was more about magic realism, but I interpreted it as a fantasy landscape showing bones and a wizard. However the author didn't like my interpretation and the painting was not used. I later heard that they went through several other covers on the book as they could not find an image or style which suited the style of the novel.

Azgar-Kumar 1982
Poster Colours
305 x 305mm
From The Chronicles of Time.
Author's own project
Previously unpublished

This was inspired by the Japanese Noh masks. The picture features the idea of conflict between good, symbolised by the Unicorn, and evil, represented by the masked man.

Prince Ombra 1984

Poster Colours
415 x 250mm
Cover for Prince Ombra by Roderick MacLeish, Pan Books

Prince Ombra is one of my favourite novels and deals with the subject of psychological conflict. The hero of the novel is a little crippled boy and the satanic adversary, Prince Ombra, makes him face himself as a crippled grown-up. Despite this the boy must defeat Prince Ombra in order to prevent wholesale nuclear war and global disaster. I think this is one of the best novels I've ever illustrated.

'Some villains can be ethereal and some can be very physical, but however you approach them you have to make them work within the context of the piece of art. If you are dealing with a villainous character, then you can create what is described in the book: perhaps some black wizard with a menacing look on his face. However, when you come to adversaries which are more intangible, perhaps more supernatural in their origin, which are maybe based on bad feelings rather than a physical entity, you then have to create something through the artwork which will

Blood Heritage 1987

Gouache
470 x 280mm
Cover for Blood Heritage by
Sheri S. Tepper, Corgi Books

The character holding the upturned goldfish bowl at the top is out for trouble. I wanted to feature the elements of the genie of the lamp, hence the stopperless bottle between the gates. The glass arch was really just a device to frame the type on the final cover.

S
B

give that feeling, it might be a mist, darkening clouds, or shadowy figures and faces in the background.

'For example there was one book I did a cover for called *Prince Ombra*. I put the warlock from the story on the cover as the central image and because the book was about a force using everything it could to attack the heroes, I reasoned that the enemy could have been nature itself. That brought in the elemental forces of fire, air, water and earth.'

Because of Stephen's Christian beliefs, he won't take on a

The Awakeners 1988
Poster Colours
530 x 310mm
Cover for The Awakeners by
Sheri S. Tepper, Bantam Press

All artists at one time or other get the opportunity to paint a procession of mad monks and this painting was my attempt. Underneath the bush on the right-hand-side can be seen a smiling bagpipe called Angus McBagpipe – one of my joke inclusions.

Still Life 1989
Gouache
455 x 275mm
Cover for Still Life by
Sheri S. Tepper, Corgi Books

With *Still Life*, the villain of the piece is not obvious. You can see the woman painting a picture but you wouldn't necessarily realise that the story's about a woman who paints pictures which come alive. This is a direct pinch from the pictures of Rene Magritte. He would paint pictures which featured a canvas where the picture behind the canvas was different from the one on it. I was pleased to be able to incorporate this idea into one of my pieces.

Groa's Other Eye 1987

Poster Colours
470 x 280mm
Cover for Groa's Other Eye by Dennis Schmidt, Orbit Books

This was the sequel to *The First Name* and the giant tree of life is changing, brightening up. The rock that the character is sitting on harks back to the floating throne of *The Non-Born King* and the flying fish have nothing whatsoever to do with the story.

commission which would mean having to paint anything connected with the satanic. 'That goes against my Christian faith. I won't touch anything connected with tarot or the occult. I was asked if I would consider painting images for a set of tarot cards a couple of years ago and I turned them down. I was also asked to do a whole series of Dennis Wheatley book covers, but I turned them down too – the Christian side of me just couldn't do it.

'I have, however, touched on aspects of the supernatural. For example Peter Valentine Timlett's series *The Seedbearers, The Power of the Serpent* and *The Twilight of the Serpent* is nominally about druids but it is actually the story of how paganism had come across from the Mediterranean and how it had been transformed into Christianity. It's about the death of the

Three Trumps Sounding 1988
Gouache
470 x 285mm
Cover for Three Trumps Sounding by Dennis Schmidt, Orbit Books

The tree of life is fading now as we reach the end of the series. The bird in the foreground and the rainbow in the water have no significance. I often add unconnected images into a painting when I feel they are needed to make the final piece work.

The Power Of The Serpent 1987
Gouache
390 x 240mm
Cover for The Power of the Serpent by Peter Valentine Timlett, Orbit Books

Following Page

Although it looks as though the druid character is about to be flattened by that rock, he isn't. The floating monolith is also not inspired by the film 2001: A Space Odyssey. The book was about druids and Stonehenge and so that formed the basis of the cover's imagery.

SB

The Seedbearers 1986
Gouache
390 x 240mm
Cover for The Seedbearers
by Peter Valentine Timlett
Orbit Books

The book featured the lost Mediterranean city of Atlantis so I included a volcano erupting to represent the destruction of the city. The survivors are escaping in the boats at the bottom left of the picture and my logo makes an appearance on the right-hand shield.

old cultures when Christianity was brought into the country by the Romans. My covers for those books took the themes and presented them in a more surrealistic and tangential way. For example, the final cover, *The Twilight of the Serpent*, showed paganism as a snake being attacked by an eagle representing the Romans. I also included pillars from different temples to show different aspects of paganism.'

5

THE WIDE HORIZON

— *Landscapes* —

If Stephen Bradbury's work has a common theme, it has to be landscapes. Each one of his paintings contains a gorgeous landscape: ice-capped mountains, rolling green hills, choppy seas, blood-red sunsets, violently exploding volcanoes – the entire range of natural scenery can be found, along with some decidedly unnatural scenery. This love and appreciation of landscapes comes from Stephen's upbringing.

Enchantment's End 1992
Gouache
440 x 270mm
Cover for Enchantment's End by Marc Alexander, Headline Books

This painting features the classic idea of emerging from a tunnel to discover a hidden valley with a ray of sunlight hitting the place for which you have been searching. I was very flattered to receive a letter from the author saying how pleased he had been with my paintings for the series of books.

The Love Rocks 1988
Gouache
180 x 350mm
Insert picture for The Grey Horse by R. A. MacAvoy
Bantam Books

Although the story was based in Ireland, the coastline on the painting is actually Cornish and the standing stones are based on a place called Lanyon Quoit, also in Cornwall.

'I've been fortunate to have lived in two of the most beautiful parts of England. I was brought up as a boy in the centre of Manchester and one of my earliest recollections is looking across the smoky rooftops, and in the distance you could just see the Derbyshire hills. For years, I couldn't work out what these strange objects were. Eventually they started knocking down all the old buildings in Manchester and moving people out into new country villages. They literally knocked down rows and rows of houses, which was criminal, and moved whole communities out into the countryside.

'The sort of streets that you see at the start of the English soap opera Coronation Street actually used to exist and I grew up in

A Blackbird In Twilight 1988

Gouache
400 x 570mm
Cover for A Blackbird in Twilight by Freda Warrington
New English Library

For some reason I was unhappy with all the paintings for Freda Warrington's Blackbird series. I think it's because of the overly cartoon style, and also because I had to pick up a series theme that had been originated by another artist. There are also a great number of different elements included in the painting.

Shadow Realm 1991

Gouache
475 x 295mm
Cover for Shadow Realm by Marc Alexander, Headline Books

I liked the idea of dolphins leading ships out of danger and so although this has nothing to do with the book, that was the image I put on the cover. I've always believed that it is best to be obscure and elusive when designing a cover. To be obvious just doesn't work as well.

Watchtower 1987
Poster Colours
473 x 330mm
Cover for Watchtower
by Elizabeth A. Lynn
Arrow Books

Watchtower was the first book in the series, *The Dancers of Arun* second and *The Northern Girl* third and I painted all three covers so that the archways would join together perfectly although the landscapes behind didn't. Despite the fact that there were months between the paintings, I managed to match the colours of the arches quite well. This is one of my favourite paintings as all the elements work perfectly. The stonework on the tower and dam was inspired by the reservoirs and dams I remembered from the Peak District.

The Dancers Of Arun 1987
Poster Colours
473 x 330mm
Cover for The Dancers of Arun
by Elizabeth A. Lynn
Arrow Books

The girl in this painting was inspired by rhythmic gymnastics using long streaming ribbons. The bird was added to give a sense of conflict to the painting.

The Northern Girl 1987
Poster Colours
473 x 330mm
Cover for The Northern Girl
by Elizabeth A. Lynn
Arrow Books

I had originally painted a face in the sky, but the publishers asked me to remove it. This was actually quite tricky as I had to scrub the original paint off after masking the rest of the picture and then air brush the sky again. The harbour in the distance is based on Mullion harbour on the Lizard peninsula in Cornwall.

Shadow's End 1995
Gouache
355 x 480mm
Cover for Shadow's End
by Sheri S. Tepper, Grafton Books

Previous Page

This was a more recent painting and I wanted to play with the geography featured on the cover. The star-shaped lake doesn't actually exist, it's been created by the angle of the painting to the mountains and the lighting. I wanted a central image so that when you see the cover, you look at the star.

S
B

Ancient Dreams 1988
Poster Colours
465 x 265mm
Cover for Ancient Dreams
by Marc Alexander
Headline Books

This painting featured an incredible and manic city-scape, almost with a toy town element to it. The character in the book is a toy maker and I think that's why I was influenced in that direction.

streets just like that. I remember that when our turn came to be moved out to the countryside it was like being stuck in a totally alien environment. However I took to it very quickly and I found these open spaces, hills and rivers a great influence. I started exploring on my bike and the overall landscape took on quite an important role in my mind.

'When I got married we lived in the High Peak area of Derbyshire which rises to 2,000 feet above sea level. We lived about 1,000 feet up, and we could see all the hills wreathed in mist above us, and the mist rolling through the valleys below and over the hilltops. We had snow covering the hills all winter and we were even able to see pure white hares that had changed

The Moon In The Water 1983
Poster Colours
295mm diameter
Cover for The Moon in the Water
by Pamela Belle, Pan Books

This was my first non-fantasy book cover. The story was set in the English Civil War. I was given the commission by Gary Day-Ellison at Pan to see how I would adapt to more general fiction and the result seemed to be quite successful.

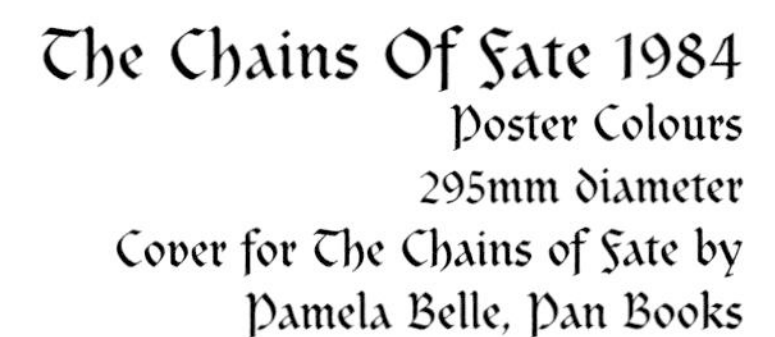

The Chains Of Fate 1984
Poster Colours
295mm diameter
Cover for The Chains of Fate by
Pamela Belle, Pan Books

This was the sequel to *The Moon in the Water*. Because of the success of my Julian May covers and also these paintings, I won Pan's Young Artist of the Year award in 1982. It was on the strength of that that I finally gave up my job as a postman and became a full-time illustrator.

S
B

The Star Bridge 1982
Poster Colours
390mm diameter
From The Chronicles of Time.
Author's own project
Previously unpublished

This picture was completed just after I had got my air brush and I was experimenting both with that technique and also with creating an image with shadows alone.

colour with the seasons, and all the other wildlife and flora changing as the seasons passed. Working as a postman, these were the sights that greeted me as I trudged along.

'Then we moved down to Cornwall, another part of the country which is very beautiful. We live on the Lizard peninsula which is noted for its impressive cliffs, rock formations and open sea. Anyone who knows the area will see that in my more recent book covers, the scenery is definitely inspired by – if not copied directly from – the areas around where I live. For example, the cover for Marion Zimmer Bradley's *The Mists of Avalon* shows the scenery looking

Grass 1989
Poster Colours
385 x 495mm
Cover for Grass
by Sheri S. Tepper
Bantam Press

Previous Page

The idea behind this novel was that the whole planet was covered in grass which was dangerous to stay in for too long and there were oases where trees grew and it was safe to stay. I used the idea of a huge crescent moon to change the impetus of the picture. If the moon was absent it would be just a very straightforward landscape. But by placing a large moon alongside a smaller one, you give the landscape a fantasy feel. The smaller moon is positioned to fall on the book's spine.

Magic Casements 1986
Gouache
465 x 295mm
Cover for Magic Casements
by Marc Alexander
Headline Books

The tower in the foreground also appeared on the cover of *Shadow Realm*. You don't ask how the water comes to be pouring out of the top of the tower. This is a fantasy book so it just is. I wanted to capture the sense of arriving somewhere, and I tried to draw the viewer into the tower.

The Reluctant Swordsman 1990

Gouache
465 x 295mm
Cover for The Reluctant Swordsman by Dave Duncan, Legend Books

The American cover for this book featured a very barbaric swordsman on the front and I went to the opposite extreme and made the landscape the prominent feature rather than the figures. The story starts with someone plunging over a waterfall and I chose that image for the background.

The Sword Of The Lictor 1990

Gouache
330 x 515mm
Cover for The Sword of the Lictor by Gene Wolfe, Legend Books

Previous page

The dams in Derbyshire which supply Manchester, Sheffield and other cities with water are absolutely massive and these inspired the dam in this picture. The rock on which the horse is standing is covered with thrift, which is a Cornish flower so the picture combines elements from different parts of the British Isles.

out towards St Michael's Mount, and the book is also set in Cornwall which helps.'

When speaking to Stephen about his work it very quickly becomes apparent that he is deeply in love with scenery and landscapes. During a break in our discussion of his work he took me on a quick tour of the area and you cannot fail to be impressed by the cliffs, the sea and the jutting rocks. There is something almost magical about standing on a cliff top looking out to sea towards the misty shadows of Cornish coastline in the far distance as sea gulls wheel and screech above you. You can see the marbled colours of the cliff-faces, the grass and thrift on the headlands, the deep blues and greens of the sea, and the vivid reds, oranges

The Coming Of Wisdom 1990
Gouache
465 x 295mm
Cover for The Coming of Wisdom by Dave Duncan, Legend Books

Here I wanted a contrasting landscape. This is a volcanic scene and, in fact, the trees on the left hand side below the cliff come from the Prince Ombra cover. There are certain elements of paintings that you can recycle lots of times.

Gods Of The New Age 1990

Gouache
470 x 285mm
Cover for Gods of the New Age by Caryl Matrisciana
Marshall Pickering Books

If you turn the painting upside down, you'll see that the reflection of the castle is a pyramid, and that there is also a claw under the water. This was an investigative book looking beneath the surface of the New Age phenomenon and so I worked on the idea that above the water all was beauty and light, and yet underneath something nasty is lurking. The floating leaves were inspired by the work of M. C. Escher.

The Earth Book Of Stormgate 3 1987

Gouache
470 x 290mm
Cover for The Earth Book of Stormgate 3 by Poul Anderson
New English Library

I'm not totally at home with science fiction and when confronted with a science fiction book my covers tend to come out being more fantasy-based with less hardware. The covers for *The Earth Book of Stormgate* are a good example of this.

The Earth Book Of Stormgate 2 1987

Gouache
470 x 290mm
Cover for The Earth Book of Stormgate 2 by Poul Anderson
New English Library

My flying fish from *Groa's Other Eye* appears again and the ship seems to have appeared on several other covers.

Pendragon's Banner 1995
Gouache
375 x 485mm
Cover for Pendragon's Banner by Helen Hollick, Mandarin Books

This was another Arthurian book, a sequel to *The Kingmaking*. The characters are looking across at Glastonbury Tor in the distance. This is quite realistically painted as the book was more of a historical romance than a fantasy.

and purples of an impressive sunset. It's hard not to be moved and inspired by Earth's natural beauty in a place like this.

Because Cornwall is a popular tourist spot, and because Stephen lives in one of the most picturesque areas of the county, he supplements his income from book commissions by painting original landscapes to sell. 'I have completed a great many Cornish landscapes and pictures of Mullion Cove, a place on the Lizard Peninsula that I am particularly fascinated and inspired by, and they are taken and sold by the Mullion Gallery. It always astonishes me that they sell so fast that they don't get a chance to get passed onto any other galleries. At the moment I'm completing two or more of these pieces a week and the Gallery is always asking for more. The last one I finished for them went into the shop at two o'clock one afternoon and had been sold by three! Incredible!'

When constructing a landscape, Stephen uses an interesting technique which is both subtle and cunning. 'What I have found is that the best way to approach a landscape is to make the viewer's eye travel into it,' he reveals. 'From a technical point of view, you therefore include pathways or entrances which lead the eye through the painting. A friend once told me that the thing about my work was that I made people want to be there; that the paintings contained an element of escape and of mystery: What is inside the castle/beyond the gates/past the

The Forest House 1993

Gouache
385 x 535mm
Cover for The Forest House
by Marion Zimmer Bradley
Michael Joseph Books

The Forest House was another book about the Romans invading Britain and the death of the druids. To represent this I placed a crow sitting atop a Roman standard with a druidic landscape below.

Tree House 1982

Poster Colours
265 x 335mm
From The Chronicles of Time.
Author's own project
Previously unpublished

This piece was inspired by Bonsai trees and the idea that someone might actually live inside them.

stone archway? A part of this is that a lot of the landscapes feature worlds that are very clean-looking places. There might be something diabolical and horrible happening in the foreground, but the worlds are completely free from pollution and there's never any litter lying around.'

In the mid-eighties, Stephen's style changed to a much harder and sharper, almost cartoon approach. 'I call it my heavy metal painting,' says Stephen. 'It's similar to the way that rock music

Encounters 1990
Gouache
360 x 500mm
Cover for Encounters
by Barbara Erskine
Michael Joseph Books

For this book of short stories I painted the same tree on the front cover as on the back cover, depicting what happens with ageing and time. The hawk was carried forward from my cover for Barbara Erskine's *Lady of Hay*.

Queen's Play 1984
Poster Colours
360 x 210mm
Cover for Queen's Play
by Dorothy Dunnett
Century Books

This cover was for a historical romance based in France. Each of the books in the series was based on a different move in chess. Therefore each of the paintings in the series featured a 'hidden' chess piece. In this painting it is under the water at the front.

The First Men In The Moon 1986

Gouache
385 x 240mm
Cover for The First Men in the Moon by H. G. Wells
Penguin Books

This is my interpretation of Wells's trip to the moon. I wanted to capture a 'Boy's Own' feel to the painting to avoid the piece becoming too sophisticated.

has different layers. On the one hand you have Pink Floyd and Yes: perhaps a more subtle approach. Then, on the other hand you have Motorhead and Iron Maiden: heavy metal rock. The bands can play the same music, the same notes, but the emphasis is completely different. With painting you can be subtle one minute and then heavier the next, depending on how you feel at the time.

'My heavy metal painting started with a cover for a re-issue of Freda Warrington's novel *A Blackbird in Darkness*. That was the second book in her Blackbird series and I hadn't done the cover for the first book, *A Blackbird in Silver*. The publishers

Men Like Gods 1987
Gouache
385 x 240mm
Cover for Men Like Gods
by H. G. Wells
Penguin Books

The cover features the idea of being transported to an alien culture. I therefore included a vintage car to provide the idea of something recognisable being placed in a totally alien environment.

A Blackbird In Darkness 1988
Poster Colours
375 x 515mm
Cover for A Blackbird in Darkness by Freda Warrington
New English Library

This was the second painting in a series. The character on the horse was being carried forward from the first cover which had not been painted by myself. My logo can be seen along with my initials on the front of the shield in the bottom right hand corner.

commissioned me to complete the covers for the remaining books in the same style as the one for the first book. I managed to adapt my normal style so that it was very similar to that of the first cover, and ended up with this more hard-edged, but rather less sophisticated approach.

The Tower Of Fear 1991
Gouache
370 x 500mm
Cover for The Tower of Fear by Glen Cook
Grafton Books

Following Page

This was another instance where the title of the book dictated what the subject matter of the cover would be. I think the piece works well with the riders charging towards the city and was designed to draw the viewer's eye there also. The shields carried by the horsemen were inspired by the Tolkien idea of the Eye of Sauron.

6

THE LIGHTS OF THEIR EYES

— Creatures —

Fantastic creatures are often featured in fantasy fiction, whether they be unicorns, dragons, chimeras or some new, nightmare monstrosity. Stephen Bradbury's paintings, however, tend to feature rather more earthbound creatures: horses, hawks, eagles and owls. This, like his love of landscapes, springs from what he sees around him.

Shadow 1989
Gouache
530 x 350mm
Cover for Shadow
by Dave Duncan
Legend Books

In this novel, all the warriors ride on the backs of giant eagles and at the bottom of the castle I have included the bars of a huge aviary where I imagined the creatures rested when not in use.

Flying Dragon 1982
Poster Colours
370mm diameter
From The Chronicles of Time.
Author's own project
Previously unpublished

This was a circular painting which I did at the same time as *The Star Bridge*. I was experimenting with circular paintings and I was quite pleased at how they turned out.

'When we first came down to Cornwall it was for a holiday and we arrived at about midnight in the pitch darkness. We really didn't know what to expect. In the morning I got up at dawn and went exploring outside, and the place where we were staying was right on the cliff. I was absolutely gobsmacked because the panorama that I saw, the huge rocks jutting out of the sea, the distant land-masses, this was the scenery that I had visualised and painted for Julian May's *The Many Coloured Land* made real. I couldn't believe it. By the end of the week's holiday I knew that I couldn't leave all this behind. So, when we got back home, we put our house up for sale and within a few months we were living here.

'If you live in the countryside – Cornwall especially – then you can't venture out without seeing buzzards, peregrine falcons, herons, you name it. Down on the Lizard Point there are the nest sites for several different birds of prey. Buzzards nest in the trees and owls can be found all over the place. When you are surrounded by all this life, then I suppose it is inevitable that they will start to appear in your work.'

Having said this, Stephen also paints dragons and other mythical monsters alongside more domesticated creatures such as cats and mice. 'I love cats, they have this wonderful way of communicating complete disdain in just a look. If you catch them unawares then they stare at you, as if to demand, "Who the hell are you looking at?"

The Earth Book Of Stormgate 1 1987
Gouache
470 x 290mm
Cover for The Earth Book of Stormgate 1 by Poul Anderson
New English Library

This series of books is about the expansion of Earthmen into the inhabited galaxy. The Earth Book is the archive of the great winged race of Ythri and the creature here is my interpretation of a winged being.

'I think it's probably easier to paint a dragon than it is to paint fur. If you take something like a mouse, you've got to put realistic bristles and fur on it. Within the time constrictions that are always present for a commercial artist, you can't put as much detail into it as perhaps it might need. Most of the time you've only got between seven and ten days to complete a painting, and so you're limited to what you can do within that time.

'Whether you are painting people, creatures or scenery, it all comes back to observation. If you look at a person, then the head is an oval shape. An arm or leg is a cylinder. A mountain might be a cone. When it comes down to it, art is really manipulating cylinders, spheres and boxes. All I'm doing is sophisticated cylinders.

'To paint a dragon, for example, you

The Revenants 1986

Poster Colours
340 x 220mm each painting
Back and front cover
for The Revenants
by Sheri S. Tepper
Corgi Books

These paintings are the back and front covers for the book. The horsemen on the back cover are riding from a city they have just set fire to and while that conflict is unfolding on the back, on the front there is a conflict between a flying creature and a unicorn which has got nothing to do with the story! You can always represent conflict by using creatures. The archway was a device I had used on previous books by the same author. This gives an identification point even though the books were not linked or even connected.

A Blackbird In Amber 1988
Gouache
400 x 575mm
Cover for A Blackbird in Amber
by Freda Warrington
New English Library

The original painting for *A Blackbird in Amber* was stolen while it was being delivered to the printers. I therefore had to repaint the whole picture from scratch, from memory, in literally a couple of days. Somewhere out there is the twin of this picture, so if you see it, let me know!

Cat-a-lyst 1992
Gouache
460 x 285mm
Cover for Cat-a-lyst
by Alan Dean Foster
Orbit Books

Following Page

The book was based in Peru and concerns a lost Incan civilisation. I used cats on the cover as the novel featured a cat as one of the prime characters.

might start with the neck. Now, the neck is a cylinder and to get a three-dimensional effect on a cylinder you make the outside of the cylinder dark and then progressively make it lighter towards the middle and then dark again towards the other edge. So that's what you do with the colours on a dragon's neck: you start with the light colours and then progressively darken the image towards the edges of the picture. This immediately gives you a solid-looking shape. Then you paint little black "u" shapes on top of your base colours to form the scales. The same basic technique applies when you paint a rock: you put the background colours on the picture first and then you start adding cracks and tonal differences on top of the basic colour.

'The difference with fur is that whereas with most painting you start with the light colours and work towards the darker end of the spectrum, here you have to work the other way round. You might paint a picture of a cat black to start with and then put the bristles on top in a lighter shade then

Codgerspace 1993

Gouache
460 x 280mm
Cover for Codgerspace
by Alan Dean Foster
Orbit Books

The book features a cyber-robotic factory where they make computer brains for robots. A technician is eating a cheese sandwich and he puts it down and a bit of it drips into the programming so that every computer brain after that moment becomes damaged. Eventually every machine in the galaxy asks the question 'Why am I here?' at the same time, and all the machines rebel against the humans. The book had a funny side and I tried to include a humorous edge to the painting.

Earthsea 1983

Poster Colours
320 x 580mm
Painting for
Realms of Fantasy
Dragon's World

Following Page

This painting was commissioned for an art book published by Dragon's World and I chose Ursula K. LeGuin's *A Wizard of Earthsea* as my subject matter. This was my first attempt at painting dragons and I am pleased with the result. There are actually three dragons in the painting: the third, which is probably the mother of the two creatures in flight, can be seen lying over a whole city in the background.

The True Game 1985

Poster Colours
340 x 220mm each painting
Front (page 118) and back (page 119) covers for
The True Game
by Sheri S. Tepper
Corgi Books

After the success of the Julian May books I started to get commissions from other publishers and *The True Game* was one of my first covers for a publisher other than Pan Books. It was the beginning of what turned out to be a huge run of covers for books by Sheri S. Tepper. The story featured battling armies ruled by lords, and the various strategies were worked out as in a huge game of chess. I therefore included a games board in the front with the pieces on, and the moves are duplicated in the background with real creatures.

The Dodos Lead The Way 1991

Gouache
300 x 425mm
From 'The Garden Series'.
Artist's own project
Previously unpublished

Dodos make wonderful fantasy pictures; they don't exist so in a way it's an immediate fantasy. What I wanted to do was to express an opinion on life and extinction but in a fantasy way. I thought dodos were an obvious creature to use, so rather than paint a picture with the gruesome aspects of extinction like rhinos being shot in Africa, I attempted a humourous slant with a parade of dodos leading to a gate with the word 'extinction' on. I loved painting the dodos and was quite sad when this picture was sold by the Portal gallery in London's Bond Street where the paintings were on display.

you might add lighter highlights to the paws or whatever. All of this has to be done in little strokes of the brush to get the effect of the individual hairs on the creature. It isn't easy.'

As well as the commissioned book covers, Stephen also completed a series of paintings for his own amusement which he has generically termed his Garden Series.

'It was the mid-eighties, and the recession was starting to bite: there were fewer commissions coming in and the publishers were offering less money for them. I was therefore looking round for things to paint in order to make money. It was on one of my trips up to London to discuss projects with various publishers that I found myself in Bond Street. There I discovered the Portal Gallery which specialises in Beryl Cooke pictures and other quirky paintings. I went in and chatted to them and they seemed very interested in taking my work on. So I started on a series of pictures which I called the Garden Series because they were all based in gardens.'

Working on his own terms, the Garden Series allowed Stephen to experiment with composition and themes that, by their very nature, were not permitted for a book cover. There were no constraints of where text had to be placed, where the spine would fall, or anything like that. 'If I wasn't doing book covers, I'd be painting like this all the time. I love the freedom of

Beliol & Diggory 1982
Poster Colours
460 x 630mm
From The Chronicles of Time.
Author's own project
Previously unpublished

Beliol is quite an amiable chap and I based him on the orc-like creatures of Tolkien, although my version is more benign. The hills in the background are the Derbyshire hills as that landscape was very familiar to me at the time.

Fire Wolf 1984
Poster Colours
420 x 255mm
Cover for Fire Wolf
by J. H. Brennan
Fontana Books

This was the first in a series of role-playing game books and it came about quite soon after the Julian May covers. The mountains and horizon are very similar to those on Julian May's books, but the foreground elements are more blatantly inspired by fantasy.

expression, to be able to paint what I want to bring over my own point.'

The title of this collection of Stephen Bradbury's fantasy artwork is *Reflections* because, for Stephen, it has been very much a case of going over the work that he has completed over the last 15 years and reflecting on what has been achieved and what has been learned.

The Crypts Of Terror 1984
Poster Colours
425 x 245mm
Cover for The Crypts of Terror by J. H. Brennan
Fontana Books

This was the follow-up to *Fire Wolf*. My idea here was to show the way into the crypts, having to pass the danger of the dragon first. The idea of a castle with a waterfall emerging from it is here as well.

Final Reflection

The world we inhabit is full of dreams
To bring them into reality – is hard, it seems
The painter with a skilful eye
Draws a landscape – creates a sky
So that others, who cannot even try
Can escape this world and learn to fly

Stephen Bradbury

'This sums up why I paint these pictures,' says Stephen about the poem above. 'It goes with the painting of the plough horse, The Plough Horse's Dream. In this picture the horse's dream is of being free from the harness and flying across the sky like a stallion, but the old farmer holding the plough is also dreaming, and his dream is of a pot of gold.

'Everybody dreams of something but most people don't attain their dreams, and whereas this horse will never be free of the harness, and the farmer will never find his pot of gold because he's missed it and he's ploughing the other side of the field now, I suppose I'm very fortunate to have ploughed my field and to have found my personal pot of gold in the process.'

These words are certainly true for Stephen Bradbury, who is both modest and self-effacing about his talent for creating the fantastic worlds that we can visit within our imaginations. Some of his work has been reflected on here and is presented for the enjoyment and appreciation of all.

The Plough Horse's Dream 1991
Gouache
425 x 300mm
From 'The Garden Series'.
Artist's own project
Previously unpublished

There are elements of Wiltshire in the background, in particular the White Horse cut into the hillside, and the landscape is deliberately very English.

Stephen Bradbury

Dove 1991
Gouache
170 x 190mm
Card design for
Westcountry
Publishing

ACKNOWLEDGMENTS

Over the years, many people have helped me in various ways and this book and the paintings within it would not have been possible without them. So thanks to:

My parents, Bill and Doreen Bradbury. My brothers Gary and Paul. Peter and Hazel Goodricke for their generosity and care. Anna and Dennis Downing for their love and support. Mike and Margaret Roberts, for introducing me to Vaughan Williams and classical music. Jan and Steve Stokes. Charles Wood. Pete and Liz Heywood at Trewince. Keith Stephens and Harold Powell at Marple. John Hall, Ivan Walton, Paul Beard, Phil Brooks and everyone at Disley P.O. Also in memory of Jack Mason.
The Portal Gallery. Agnes and Tony Lewis at Mullion Gallery.
In publishing: Ian Hughes, Peter Cotton, Janette Dimond, John Munday, Bruce Low, Dennis Barker, Alan Spain, Rob Hollingsworth, Mike Bates, Liz Laczynska, Eddi Edwards, Dave Grogan, Richard Evans and the late Steve Abbis.
A very special thanks to Gary Day Ellison.
David J. Howe and photographer Tony Mann for their help with this book.
The music of Yes, Pink Floyd, The Enid, Neil Young, 'et al' Rock groups who have kept me company during the long, lonely hours of painting...
One day I'll do an album cover.............please!!
Finally, to the Lord for the very special gift of painting.